Come, Lord Jesus

DEVOTIONS FOR
THE HOME

ADVENT

CHRISTMAS   EPIPHANY

Susan Briehl

Augsburg Fortress
Minneapolis

COME, LORD JESUS
Devotions for Advent, Christmas, Epiphany

Editors: Samuel Torvend, Linda Parriott
Cover design: Circus Design
Interior design: Marti Naughton
Interior art: Brian Jensen

Library of Congress Cataloging-in-Publication Data

Briehl, Susan, 1952–
    Come Lord Jesus : devotions for Advent, Christmas, Epiphany /
Susan Briehl.
        p.   cm.
    Includes bibliographical references.
    ISBN 0-8066-2982-7 (alk. paper)
    1. Advent—Prayer-books and devotions—English. 2. Christmas—Prayer-books and devotions—English. 3. Epiphany—Prayer-books and devotions—English. I. Title.
    BV40.B74   1996
    242' .33—dc20   96-21186
                                                                                              CIP

The paper used in this publication meets the minimum requirements of American National Standard for Information Sciences—Permanence of Paper for Printed Library Materials, ANSI Z329.48-1984.   ∞™

Printed in the U.S.A.   ISBN 0-8066-2982-7   10-29827

                                        5   6   7   8

Table of Contents

How to use this book

This small book is filled with many diverse treasures that will lead the household of faith through Advent, Christmas, and Epiphany. It can be used in different ways depending upon the particular needs and daily schedule of the household. Use whatever works well in your home. Adapt what is presented here to your pattern of life. Enrich the suggestions of this book with customs, prayers, and songs that are cherished in your home.

Some people may want to use this book primarily as a source for scripture reading and reflection. To that end, a *meditation* has been included for each week and festival day. It is inspired by the *scripture readings* that are suggested for use throughout the week. In addition to the weekly or festival meditation, you will find a gathering of *poems:* some are old, others are newly-composed. Each one reflects the poet's perception of the season or suggested scripture reading.

The Christmas season is one of the few times in the year when many people do not hesitate to sing beloved carols and hymns with friends and family. For each week and day, a *song* is printed for singing in the household. In the back of the book, an index is printed that lists many familiar alternate tunes.

In some homes, there is time for a quiet and leisurely reading of scripture or reflection on poetry. But the Christmas season also brings much activity to other households. If that is true of your home, then use the *table prayer* when you gather for a meal. This is a brief and simple way to mark the changing of the weeks and seasons. If time allows, have one person at the table read a portion of scripture or one of the brief prayers included in this book.

Gathering for a brief daily or weekly prayer can take place in different settings. In some homes, people gather throughout Advent around the burning candles of the wreath. During the Twelve Days of Christmas, a family may gather around the Christmas tree. Some households will gather for prayer during Christmas time or Epiphany at the nativity or manger scene. Wherever you gather for prayer, use the *blessings* that may begin or be the center of your prayer: the blessing of the Advent wreath, the lighting of the Christmas tree, the placement of the figures in a nativity scene.

In many homes with children, certain seasonal customs become cherished treasures that are handed on from one generation to another. This book includes *holiday customs* from around the world that set forth visually the meaning of the weekly and festival scripture readings. Children are welcome to participate in these customs. In addition, this book includes *prayers for young children* throughout the week under the heading: "Advent/Christmas/Epiphany prayer for children." Since many are easily memorized, these prayers can carry the meaning of the week or season throughout the day. They may be especially useful at bedtime.

The great gift of this book is that it invites the use of the senses. One can read, hear, sing, taste, touch, and see the presence of Christ in the home throughout the weeks of Advent, the Twelve Days of Christmas, and the special days that mark Epiphany.

The prayer of Christians

One of the oldest prayers of the Christian community is also the title of this book: Come, Lord Jesus. In Aramaic, the language that Jesus spoke, one word—Maranatha—said two things. It was a prayer for help in time of need: Come, Lord, save us. It was also used as a joyous and confident welcome to the risen Christ: Come, Lord Jesus, be our guest.

In the weeks of Advent, the Christian people practice together God's gift of hope. We offer thanksgiving to God for the gift of the Son born at Bethlehem among the poor. We welcome Christ today in his holy word and holy supper, in the waters of baptism, and in the faith of our brothers and sisters. And we look for that day when he will come again and mercifully gather us into our eternal home.

Be welcome, then, to this gathering of words and signs that welcomes Christ in the home through the Christmas season. Use this book and its many treasures as if it were a prayer that God would come among us and be our guest.

Advent

A shoot shall come out from the stump of Jesse,
and a branch shall grow out of his roots.
The spirit of the Lord shall rest upon him.

ISAIAH 11:1–2

The First Week in Advent

Come, let us walk in the light of the Lord
ISAIAH 2:5

Advent means "to come." During this season we prepare for three advents. The first is the coming of Jesus two thousand years ago. We remember the faithful people who waited and watched for God's promised Messiah: Abraham and Sarah, Moses, Miriam, and Aaron, David the king, Isaiah the prophet, Elizabeth and Zechariah, Simeon, Anna, and many more. They lived by faith, holding fast to God's promise.

The second advent is the coming of Christ among us now. Every day is an advent because Jesus is Emmanuel, God-always-with-us. Christ comes to us in the waters of baptism, with the bread and wine of his holy meal, through the Word of God, and in the community of faith. Christ surprises us by coming at the times, in the places, and through the people we least expect, startling us with grace and bringing us new life.

The third and final advent is yet to come. No one knows the day or the hour. Christ will come at the end of time, gathering God's beloved people into one embrace and mending with mercy what sin has torn apart. As with the coming of Christmas Day, we cannot make it happen sooner because we are eager, nor can we delay it because we are not ready. However, we can be awake and alert, standing on tiptoe, wide-eyed and watchful, ready to receive him whenever he comes.

Even as we prepare to celebrate the birth of Jesus, we confess the deepest truth about him: Christ has died. Christ is risen. Christ will come again. So we pray with hopeful hearts, "Come, Lord Jesus. Surprise us with life that has no end, life that comes from you."

Angels gather.
The rush of mad air
cyclones through.
Wing tips brush the
hair, a million
strands
stand; waving black anemones.
Hosannahs crush the
shell's ear tender, and
tremble
down clattering
to the floor.
Harps sound,
undulate their
sensuous meanings.
Hallelujah! Hallelujah!
You
beyond the door.

MAYA ANGELOU

HYMN

Come, thou long-expected Jesus, born to set thy people free;
from our fears and sins release us; let us find our rest in thee.
Israel's strength and consolation, hope of all the earth thou art,
dear desire of ev'ry nation, joy of ev'ry longing heart.

Born thy people to deliver, born a child, and yet a king;
born to reign in us forever, now thy gracious kingdom bring.
By thine own eternal Spirit rule in all our hearts alone;
by thine all-sufficient merit raise us to thy glorious throne.

Tune: JEFFERSON—*other tunes are noted in the index*

FOR READING THROUGHOUT THE WEEK

Isaiah 2:1–5	Matthew 24:36–44
Isaiah 64:1–9	Mark 13:24–37
Jeremiah 33:14–16	Luke 21:25–36

A PRAYER FOR THE WEEK

Lord Jesus,
we do not lack any spiritual gift as we wait for your coming.
Keep us awake and help us use our gifts
to serve those who look for the dawn of your justice and mercy. Amen

TABLE PRAYER

Maranatha!
Come, Lord Jesus, be our guest; let these gifts to us be blest.
Keep us always in your sight; be our joy, our hearts' delight.
Amen

ADVENT PRAYER FOR CHILDREN

God in the night
God at my right
God all the day
God with me stay
God in my heart
Never depart
God with thy might
Keep us in light
Through this dark night.
Amen

THE ADVENT WREATH

One of the best known customs for the season is the Advent wreath. The wreath and winter candle-lighting in the midst of growing darkness strengthen some of the Advent images found in the Bible. The unbroken circle of greens is clearly an image of evergreen life, a victory wreath, the crown of Christ, or the wheel of time itself. Christians use the wreath as a sign that Christ reaches into our time to lead us to the light of ever-lasting life. The four candles mark the progress of the four weeks of Advent and the growth of light. Sometimes the wreath is embellished with natural dried flowers or fruit. Its evergreen branches lead the household to the evergreen Christmas tree. In many homes, the family gathers for prayer around the wreath.

LIGHTING THE ADVENT WREATH

The lighting of the wreath may begin Advent prayer in the home.
Use this blessing when lighting the first candle.

Blessed are you, O Lord our God, ruler of the universe.
You call all nations to walk in your light
and to seek your ways of justice and peace,
for the night is past, and the dawn of your coming is near.
Bless us as we light the first candle of this wreath.
Rouse us from sleep,
that we may be ready to greet our Lord when he comes
and welcome him into our hearts and homes,
for he is our light and our salvation.
Blessed be God forever.

THE JESSE TREE

The Jesse tree first appeared in thirteenth century stained glass church windows. The images of Christ's ancestors caught the attention of many Christians. In its origin, the tree represented the lineage of Jesus beginning with Adam and Eve as described in Luke. It is an image of the tree of life in Eden, the tree of Christ's cross, the healing tree of the Book of Revelation, and the Christmas tree that proclaims the branch of Jesse, the righteous shoot.

Today the physical images of Christ's ancestors have been replaced by symbols: globe (the creation of the world), apple (Adam and Eve in the garden, at the tree of life), ark or rainbow (the flood; the covenant with Noah), ram (Isaac, a figure of the Christ; covenant with Abraham), coat of many colors (Joseph, the favored son who saved his family from famine), tablets of the Law (Ten Commandments; covenant with Israel), key and crown (house of David; royal city of Bethlehem), scroll (the prophets who reminded the people of their covenant with God), shell and water (John the Baptist; baptism in the Jordan), hammer and square (Joseph the carpenter), lily (Mary), chi-rho (the first two Greek letters of the word Christ).

The Jesse tree can be decorated in many ways. The ornaments might be designed by children. You can make the Jesse tree a project that lasts through the entire season, adding a symbol for one ancestor in the faith each day. The tree would then become the fully decorated Christmas tree at the end of Advent. Or you could have a Jesse tree party. Give each guest a biblical character and appropriate scripture citation and the freedom to create a symbol. Have plenty of string and paper and glue, glitter, fabric scraps, and imaginative miscellany on hand, as well as Bibles.

PRAYER AT THE JESSE TREE

Use this brief prayer when you gather at the Jesse tree. Each person responds with the words printed in bold.

In the garden you gave us the tree of life.
Lord, have mercy.
On the tree of the cross you forgave us our sins.
Christ, have mercy.
You bring hope to all who cling to the new branch of Jesse's tree.
Lord, have mercy.

THE MANGER SCENE

Here is a household practice that begins in Advent and continues through the Twelve Days of Christmas until the celebration of the Epiphany on January 6. It is a custom that immerses children in the story and makes them participants. The family places a stable somewhere in the center of the house, perhaps close to where the Christmas tree will be placed. The empty manger, various animals, and an inn keeper can be there as well. The shepherds and sheep are on a "hillside" in another room. Mary and Joseph are in "Nazareth." The three kings are in the easternmost room of the house. The infant Jesus is hidden.

During Advent the figures move. Mary and Joseph begin their journey to Bethlehem. The children may move them down the hallway, across rooms. The figures can move a little every week or every day. On Christmas Eve the Christ Child and the angels appear while the shepherds rush from the hillside to Bethlehem. On Christmas Day morning the shepherds may stay by the manger or return to the hillside. Then the three kings begin their twelve-day journey from the east following the star. A star and the kings may move from room to room. They arrive on January 6, the Epiphany, bearing gifts for the children in the family. They remain until the Transfiguration.

BLESSING OF THE MANGER SCENE

Use this blessing when figures are added to the manger scene.

O Lord our God,
with Mary and Joseph,
angels and shepherds,
and the animals in the stable,
we gather around your Son, born for us.
Bless us with your holy presence
and inspire us to help those who have no place to dwell.
Be with us that we might share Christ's love with all the world,
for he is our light and salvation.
Glory in heaven and peace on earth,
now and forever.
Amen

The Second Week in Advent

Shower, O heavens, from above,
and let the skies rain down righteousness;
let the earth open, that salvation may spring up.

ISAIAH 45:8

In the northern hemisphere, the days grow shorter and the nights deeper during these weeks of watchful waiting. By the frail and flickering light of the candles on the Advent wreath, we pray, "Come, Lord Jesus. Come reign among us with peace and mercy." These little flames are signs of hope. Their dancing light reminds us that the light of Christ shines in the darkness, and the darkness will not overcome it.

In the southern hemisphere, December days are warm, and the land is being prepared for planting. Here, too, is a sign of Advent hope. In the words of a Spanish Advent carol: "All earth is hopeful, the Savior comes at last!" Even the soil seems to sing of what is to come: work with a just reward, an abundant harvest so none will hunger, and peace throughout the land. "Furrows lie open for God's creative task." The whole creation is waiting and cries, "Come, Lord Jesus."

In Christ Jesus, God is doing something new: planting the seeds of the new creation and leading us toward a harvest of justice and peace. "Prepare the way of the Lord," John the Baptist cries, "make his paths straight" (Matt. 3:3b). We are invited to live and labor in hope. When we tend the earth with care, serve our neighbors in love, and do the things that make for peace, we welcome God's reign among us. For Christ comes to us in our neighbor who is hungry and weary and waiting for mercy. We watch with hope for signs of Christ's presence and eagerly join in God's creative task of making all things new.

The wilderness and the dry land shall be glad,
    the desert shall rejoice and blossom;
like the crocus it shall blossom abundantly,
    and rejoice with joy and singing.

The glory of Lebanon shall be given to it,
    the majesty of Carmel and Sharon.
They shall see the glory of the Lord,
    the majesty of our God.

Then the eyes of the blind shall be opened,
    and the ears of the deaf unstopped;
then the lame shall leap like a deer,
    and the tongue of the speechless sing for joy.
For waters shall break forth in the wilderness,
    and streams in the desert.

And the ransomed of the Lord shall return,
    and come to Zion with singing;
everlasting joy shall be upon their heads;
    they shall obtain joy and gladness,
and sorrow and sighing shall flee away.

ISAIAH 35: 1, 2, 5, 6, 10

HYMN

When the King shall come again all his pow'r revealing,
splendor shall announce his reign, life and joy and healing;
earth no longer in decay, hope no more frustrated;
this is God's redemption day longingly awaited.

In the desert trees take root fresh from his creation;
plants and flow'rs and sweetest fruit join the celebration;
rivers spring up from the earth, barren lands adorning;
valleys, this is your new birth, mountains, greet the morning!

Strengthen feeble hands and knees, fainting hearts, be cheerful!
God who comes for such as these seeks and saves the fearful;
deaf ears, hear the silent tongues sing away their weeping;
blind eyes, see the lifeless ones walking, running, leaping.

Tune: GAUDEAMUS PARITER *(Come, you faithful, raise the strain)*

FOR READING THROUGHOUT THE WEEK

Isaiah 11:1–10	Matthew 3:1–12
Isaiah 40:1–11	Mark 1:1–8
Malachi 3:1–4	Luke 3:1–6

A PRAYER FOR THE WEEK

God our shepherd, gather us as lambs in your arms.
Forgive our sins so that we may rejoice in your coming. Amen

TABLE PRAYER

Maranatha!
Come, Lord Jesus, be our guest; let these gifts to us be blest.
May there be a goodly share on every table everywhere.
Amen

ADVENT PRAYER FOR CHILDREN

Use this prayer with hands open and palms up.

Here I wait in quiet hope
that you will come,
water the field of my heart,
and make your love blossom.
Amen

LIGHTING THE ADVENT WREATH

*Use this blessing when lighting the first two candles of the
Advent wreath.*

Blessed are you, O Lord our God, ruler of the universe.
John the Baptist calls all people to prepare the Lord's way
for the kingdom of heaven is near.
Bless us as we light the candles on this wreath.
Baptize us with the fire of your Spirit,
that we may be a light shining in the darkness
welcoming others as Christ has welcomed us,
for he is our light and our salvation.
Blessed be God forever.

PLANTING SPRING IN WINTER

Plant small bulbs—paper whites or narcissus—in a clay pot filled with
rich soil. Set it near a sunny window. During Advent watch the shoots
emerge. During the Twelve Days of Christmas, delicate white flowers
will bloom and fill the room with a sweet fragrance, a reminder of God's
promise to make all things new in Christ Jesus.

Third Week in Advent

Be strong, do not fear! Here is your God.

ISAIAH 35:4

John the Baptist is like a rooster, that irritating barnyard alarm clock who interrupts our sleep at the break of dawn calling, "Cock-a-doodle-doo. Wake up! The sun is rising. The light has come." We would rather turn over, snuggle down into the blankets, and sleep a little longer, but the rooster is as insistent as an alarm clock: "Wake up, or you will miss the morning."

What will we miss if we do not listen to John the Baptist? We will miss the coming of Jesus who already stands among us. Does someone stand beside you who longs to be held or healed? Is there one waiting for your forgiveness? Shake the sleepiness from your head. Open your arms. When you embrace with love the one who waits, you will see that the Light has come.

Is there someone knocking at the door, weary and in need of rest, afraid and in need of safety? Let your ears hear. Swing wide the door of your home and your heart. Christ is knocking.

Is there one among you, whom you do not know, who is hungry or cold? Rise to greet the stranger. Open your hands to share your bread, for where we serve our neighbor, there Christ comes.

John the Baptist calls to us this day. Do not turn over and go back to sleep, but turn toward the Light and let your lives be turned around. One is coming, indeed is already among us, who is the Dayspring, the dawn of God's new day, Christ the Lord.

i thank You God for most this amazing
day:for the leaping greenly spirits of trees
and a blue true dream of sky;and for everything
which is natural which is infinite which is yes

(i who have died am alive again today,
and this is the sun's birthday;this is the birth
day of life and of love and wings:and of the gay
great happening illimitably earth)

how should tasting touching hearing seeing
breathing any—lifted from the no
of all nothing—human merely being
doubt unimaginable You?

(now the ears of my ears awake and
now the eyes of my eyes are opened)

e.e. cummings

HYMN

Hark, the glad sound! The Savior comes, the Savior promised long;
Let ev'ry heart prepare a throne and ev'ry voice a song.

He comes the pris'ners to release, in Satan's bondage held.
The gates of brass before him burst, the iron fetters yield.

He comes the broken heart to bind, the bleeding soul to sure,
and with the treasures of his grace to'enrich the humble poor.

Tune: CHESTERFIELD—*other tunes are noted in the index*

FOR READING THROUGHOUT THE WEEK

Isaiah 35:1–10	Matthew 11:2–11
Isaiah 61:1–11	John 1:6–8, 19–28
Zephaniah 3:14–20	Luke 3:7–18

A PRAYER FOR THE WEEK

Lord Jesus, you continue to do great things for us.
Give us your gift of peace as we await your coming.
Amen

ADVENT PRAYER FOR CHILDREN

Use this prayer and follow the actions as you are able.

Open my eyes to see your light.
Open my hands to receive your bread.
Open my ears to hear your word.
Open my mouth to speak your love.

TABLE PRAYER

Maranatha!
Come, Lord Jesus, be our guest; let these gifts to us be blest.
Guide us on the servant's way; lead us to your dawning day.
Amen

LIGHTING THE ADVENT WREATH

Use this prayer when the lighting the three candles of the Advent wreath.

Blessed are you, O Lord our God, ruler of the universe.
Your prophets spoke of a day when the desert would blossom
and waters would break forth in the wilderness.
Bless us as we light the candles on this wreath.
Strengthen our hearts
as we prepare for the coming of the Lord.
May he give water to all who thirst,
for he is our light and our salvation.
Blessed be God forever.

LAS POSADAS

In many Hispanic communities, Las Posadas ("lodgings" or "shelters") begins this week, nine days before Christmas. Each night a group of "travelers" goes from door to door, knocking and asking for a place to stay, as Mary and Joseph once did. Each night they are turned away when the people within the house say, "There is no room." On Christmas Eve, the travelers knock at a final door, which opens to receive them with joy and celebration. In this way, each year, the community enters anew the story of God's hospitality to them in Christ and hears Christ's call to offer the same hospitality to the stranger, the traveler, the refugee, and all in need of posada.

While Las Posadas is celebrated in Hispanic communities, it is becoming a popular practice in other communities as well. Between December 16 and 24, families or small groups gather one or more evenings to mark the journey of Mary and Joseph to Bethlehem. This is much like a "progressive party" in which the family or group visits one or more homes. They ask to come in, but a rude voice says there is no room. Then the visitors either respond that Mary is about to give birth to the king of heaven or they sing an Advent carol foretelling his birth. Immediately the door is opened, and everyone is welcomed into a great party of traditional holiday food and singing.

The Fourth Week in Advent

O come, O Dayspring, come with cheer;
O Sun of Justice, now dear near.

All in a row they stood, each one smaller than the next, four wooden Matrushka dolls, made to come apart in the middle and nest inside each other. Their eyes, noses, and mouths were painted black. Their flowered dresses and babushkas, the scarves upon their heads, were hues of red and gold.

The child, whose grandma owned these dolls, had given each a name and a part to play in a most beloved story: Gabriel, Joseph, Mary, and Elizabeth. The largest was the angel who said again and again, "Don't be afraid, Joseph. Don't be afraid, Mary. You don't have to be afraid. God is with you."

They knew their parts perfectly, these Russian dolls, as the child moved them through the story. Joseph woke from his dream to give Mary a hug. Gabriel entered Nazareth to bring good news. Mary rushed to the hill country to visit Elizabeth. When Mary and Elizabeth greeted one another, they danced around together, making gentle, rattling music. Inside the Matrushka doll named Elizabeth was an even smaller one named John. He was leaping for joy inside his mother.

"You have brought my Lord to me," Elizabeth said, for hidden deep within the doll named Mary was the tiniest doll of all. His name was Jesus. Because Mary bore Jesus, she is called Theotokos, a Greek word meaning God-bearer. Christ still comes to us hidden in weakness. He comes wounded by death and risen to life. He comes to call the lowly blessed and to make the little ones leap for joy. We who have received him through water and word, bread and wine, are called to be Christ-bearers in the world. "Come, Lord Jesus," we pray, "Come to us. Come through us."

There stood in heaven a linden tree,
But, tho' 'twas honey-laden,
All angels cried, "No bloom shall be
Like that of one fair maiden."

Sped Gabriel on winged feet,
And passed through bolted portals
In Nazareth, a maid to greet,
Blest o'er all other mortals.

"Hail Mary!" quoth the angel mild.
"Of womankind the fairest:
The Virgin aye shalt thou be styled,
A babe although thou bearest."

"So be it!" God's handmaiden cried,
"According to thy telling."
Whereon the angel smartly hied
Up homeward to his dwelling.

This tiding filled his friends with glee:
'Twas passed from one to other,
That 'twas Mary, and none but she.
And God would call her mother.

DUTCH CAROL

HYMN

During the final days of Advent, December 17–23,
an O-Antiphon is sung each day.

December 17

O come, O Wisdom from on high,
who governs all things tenderly;
to us the path of knowledge show,
and teach us in her ways to go. *Refrain*

December 18

> O come, O come, great Lord of might,
> > who to your tribes on Sinai's height
> in ancient times once gave the law,
> > in cloud and majesty, and awe. *Refrain*

December 19

> O come, O Flower of Jesse's Root,
> > before whom all the world stands mute.
> We trust your mighty power to save,
> > and give us victory o'er the grave. *Refrain*

December 20

> O come, O Key of David, come,
> > and open wide our heavenly home;
> make safe the way that leads on high,
> > and close the path to misery. *Refrain*

December 21

> O come, O Dayspring, come with cheer;
> > O Sun of Justice, now draw near.
> Disperse the gloomy clouds of night,
> > and death's dark shadow put to flight. *Refrain*

December 22

> O come, O Keystone,
> > come and bind in one the hearts of humankind.
> Come bid our sad divisions cease,
> > and be for us the King of peace. *Refrain*

December 23

> O come, O come, Emmanuel,
> > and ransom captive Israel,
> that mourns in lonely exile here
> > until the Son of God appear. *Refrain*

Refrain

> *Rejoice! Rejoice! Emmanuel shall come to you, O Israel.*

FOR READING THROUGHOUT THE WEEK

Isaiah 7:10–16	Matthew 1:18–25
2 Samuel 7:1–16	Luke 1:26–38
Micah 5:2–5	Luke 1:39–55

A PRAYER FOR THE WEEK

Give ear, O Shepherd of Israel, you who lead Joseph like a flock.
Restore us, O God; let your face shine on us, that we may be saved.
Amen

ADVENT PRAYER FOR CHILDREN

*Whether you put an angel on the Christmas tree or over the bed,
use this prayer in the last days of Advent and during Christmastime:*

Angel sent by God to guide me,
be my light and walk beside me;
be my guardian and protect me
on the paths of life direct me.

TABLE PRAYER

Maranatha!
Come, Lord Jesus, be our guest; let these gifts to us be blest.
Deep within us come to dwell that we might all your goodness tell.
Amen

LIGHTING THE ADVENT WREATH

Use this prayer when lighting the four candles of the Advent wreath.

Blessed are you, O Lord our God, ruler of the universe.
In your Son, Emmanuel,
you have shown us your light
and saved us from the power of sin.
Bless us as we light the candles on this wreath.
Increase our longing for your presence,
that at the celebration of your Son's birth
his Spirit might dwell anew in our midst,
for he is our light and our salvation.
Blessed be God forever.

CHRISTOPOSOMO

Here is an Advent/Christmas custom from Greece. Christoposomo
(Christ-bread) is a light, fragrant bread made with milk, butter, white
flour, and yeast. Honey sweetens it, four eggs make it rich. A generous
teaspoon of crushed anise seed gives it a distinctive flavor and aroma.
Sometimes a coin, wrapped in foil, is hidden in the bread. The person
who finds the coin is invited to give a blessing to all who share the
bread. Use a bread recipe that includes all the ingredients mentioned
here. Before it is baked, this round loaf is always topped with a large
cross made from ropes of dough, a reminder that the crib and the cross
cannot be separated. If you bake a few loaves, they may be given away as
Christmas gifts to friends, relatives, or a center that serves food to the
poor and homeless.

Christmas

The Word became flesh and lived among us,
and we have seen his glory,
the glory as of a father's only son,
full of grace and truth.

JOHN 1:14

Christmas Eve

To you is born this day a Savior.
LUKE 2:11

On a low, simple table at the center of their home, a family places a wooden stable and surrounds it with straw. Delicate figures, carved by hand, tell the story of Christmas. Mary and Joseph watch over the baby wrapped in swaddling cloths and lying in the manger. Shepherds and sheep draw near to see this wonder that has happened. With the shepherds stand other figures dressed in traditional Polish peasant clothing. They represent the members of the family living in this house.

This family knows that the angel's words are spoken to them: "To *you* is born this day a Savior, who is the Messiah, the Lord." These words are spoken to us, too. This gift is given to us. This night we leave the fields of our daily lives, the places where we work and go to school and play with friends. We travel through the night to the manger. Or better, the one who was born in a manger comes to us, crucified and risen from the dead.

With eager hearts we pray, "Come, Lord Jesus." With open, empty hands we stand at the table, as if with the shepherds, peasants in Poland, and faithful people in every land. We receive from God the gift of life, the very presence of our Savior, wrapped in bread and wine. "Given for you," the messenger of God says. "Amen," we reply, "It is true."

Leaving the table, our sins forgiven and our hope renewed, we are sent back to the fields, back to our ordinary lives. We return, as the shepherds did, praising God and telling everyone the good news of great joy. "Glory to God in the highest, " we sing with the angels, "and peace to God's people on earth."

Infant holy, infant lowly, for his bed a cattle stall;
oxen lowing, little knowing Christ the child is Lord of all.
Swiftly winging, angels singing, bells are ringing, tidings bringing:
Christ the child is Lord of all! Christ the child is Lord of all!

Flocks were sleeping, shepherds keeping vigil till the morning new
saw the glory, heard the story, tidings of a Gospel true.
Thus rejoicing, free from sorrow, praises voicing, greet the morrow:
Christ the child was born for you!
Christ the child was born for you!

POLISH CAROL

HYMN

Your little ones, dear Lord are we, and come your lowly bed to see;
enlighten ev'ry soul and mind, that we the way to you may find.

With songs we hasten you to greet, and kiss the ground before your feet.
Oh, blessed hour, oh, sweetest night that gave you birth, our soul's delight.

Oh, draw us wholly to you, Lord, and to us all your grace accord;
true faith and love to us impart, that we may hold you in our heart.

Until at last we too proclaim, with all your saints, your glorious name;
in paradise our songs renew, and praise you as the angels do.

Tune: HERR KOMMER DINE ARME SMAA—*other tunes are noted in the index*

FOR READING ON CHRISTMAS EVE

Isaiah 9:2–7   Psalm 96   Luke 2:1–20

A PRAYER FOR CHRISTMAS

Almighty God,
you enlighten the darkness with the true Light.
In the days ahead, help us walk in Christ's light,
and on the last day awaken us to the brightness of his glory.
Amen

CHRISTMAS PRAYER FOR CHILDREN

Be near me, Lord Jesus; I ask you to stay
close by me forever and love me, I pray.
Bless all the dear children in your tender care
and fit us for heaven to live with you there.

TABLE PRAYER

With joy and gladness we feast upon your love, O God.
You have come among us in Jesus, your Son,
and your presence now graces this table.
May Christ dwell in us that we might bear his love to all the world,
for he is Lord forever and ever.
Amen

THE CHRISTMAS TREE

In Denmark the Christmas tree is not cut and brought into the house
until December 23 or 24. Sometimes the parents decorate the tree and
keep it hidden behind closed doors. After supper on Christmas Eve the
doors are opened, revealing a tree illumined with real candles. Everyone
holds hands and dances in a line through the rooms of the house. Then
they circle around the candle-lit tree, singing carols. Before opening
gifts, they sing one last song, repeating it many times:

Now it is Christmas again.
Now it is Christmas again.
Christmas lasts until Easter.
No. It is not true.
No. It is not true.
In between comes the fast.

LIGHTING THE CHRISTMAS TREE

Use this prayer when you first illumine the tree
or when you gather at the tree.

God our Creator,
we praise you for this Christmas tree.
It is a sign of your everlasting, evergreen presence.
It is a sign of the reign of heaven,
sheltering the creatures of the earth under its open arms.
It is a sign of the cross,
shining with the light of your grace and mercy.

Gracious God,
let your blessing come upon us
as we illumine this tree.
Send us your Son,
the tender shoot of Jesse,
who brings us light and life.

May all who stand in its light
eagerly welcome the true Light which never fades.
We ask this through Christ our Lord.
Amen

BLESSING OF CHRISTMAS GIFTS

Use this prayer before you open Christmas presents.

Blessed be your name, O God,
you are the source of every blessing.
From your hand, we receive the good gifts
of life, health, and salvation.
As we give and receive these presents,
bless us with hearts thankful for the birth of your Son.
May our opening of these gifts lead us
to share our love, faith, and goods with the poor and needy.
Blessed be God forever.

LUMINARIA

Here is a way to welcome people to your home with small Christ lights, a custom in Mexico and the Southwest. Fill small brown paper bags one-third full of sand or dirt. Set in each bag a candle stub or votive candle. Place them outside on your porch or along the pathway to your home. The candles can be lighted each evening during the Twelve Days of Christmas to illumine the way to your door, a sign of hospitality to friends and strangers alike who come for the joy of shared food, song, and conversation. Lanterns made from tin cans also work. Decorate them by pounding holes in the cans with a hammer and nail. The light of the candle shines through the design you have created with the holes.

Christmas Day

The light shines in the darkness, and the darkness did not overcome it.
JOHN 1:5

In the historic heart of Albuquerque, now called Old Town, low, adobe buildings stand facing a common ground, the original town square. Each year on Christmas Eve their flat roofs are lined with luminaria: small brown paper bags, each weighted with sand and holding a burning candle, whose light glows golden against the midnight sky.

Standing in the center of Old Town Square on this silent and holy night, one is surrounded by a halo of light. It is a beacon for the lost, beauty for the brokenhearted, comfort to those chilled by grief or guilt or shame. In the deepest part of the night, the light embraces all who gather outside the door of the church and await the dawn of redeeming grace.

When Christmas day is dawning, there is no need of glowing luminaria. The buildings of Old Town are pink with morning light, all darkness banished by the advent of the sun. Yet, by the light of day we face the truth that nights of fear remain. We admit that sickness and sorrow still abound, that some are filled with good things while others are sent away empty, that nations are at war, and death knocks always at life's door.

Into our nights of fear God speaks Light. Into the darkness of death God speaks Life. Into a wounded world God speaks Jesus. We who receive him become children of God, bearing witness to the Light who comes with grace for all people. Like the luminaria, we are illumined from within by the presence of Christ. Loving one another with the love we first received from God, we declare, "The light shines in the darkness, and the darkness did not overcome it."

Tell again the Christmas story:
Christ is born in all His glory!

Baby laid in manger dark,
Lighting ages with the spark
Of innocence that is the Child
Trusting all within His smile.

Tell again the Christmas story
With the halo of His glory:
Halo born of humbleness
By the breath of cattle blest,
By the poverty of stall
Where a bed of straw is all,
By a door closed at the inn
Only men of means get in
By a door closed to the poor,
Christ born on earthen floor
in a stable with no lock—
Yet kingdoms tremble at the shock
Of a king in swaddling clothes
At an address no one knows
Because there is no painted sign—
Nothing but a star divine,
Nothing but a halo bright
About His young head in the night,
Nothing but the wondrous light
Of innocence that is the Child
Trusting all within His smile.

Mary's Son of golden star:
Wise Men journey from afar.
Mary's Son in manger born:
Music of the Angel's horn.
Mary's Son in straw and glory:

Wonder of the Christmas story!

LANGSTON HUGHES

HYMN

What child is this, who, laid to rest, on Mary's lap is sleeping?
Whom angels greet with anthems sweet while shepherds watch are keeping?
This, this is Christ the king, whom shepherds guard and angels sing;
Haste, haste to bring him laud, the babe, the son of Mary!

Why lies he in such mean estate where ox and ass are feeding?
Good Christian, fear; for sinners here the silent Word is pleading.
Nails, spear shall pierce him through, the cross be borne for me, for you;
Hail, hail the Word made flesh, the babe, the son of Mary!

So bring him incense, gold, and myrrh; come, peasant, king, to own him.
The King of kings salvation brings; let loving hearts enthrone him.
Raise, raise the song on high, the virgin sings her lullaby;
Joy, joy, for Christ is born, the babe, the son of Mary!

Tune: GREENSLEEVES

FOR READING ON CHRISTMAS DAY

Isaiah 52:7–10   Psalm 98   John 1:1–14

A PRAYER FOR CHRISTMAS DAY

Lord God,
may your Word become flesh through our lives
so that others may see him in our love for each other,
our service to the needy, and our care for the little ones of this earth.
Amen

CHRISTMAS PRAYER FOR CHILDREN

Here is the stable
where Jesus was born
and was laid in the manger
that first Christmas morn.

And Mary and Joseph
and cattle and sheep
smiled down on the baby
and watched him, asleep.

TABLE PRAYER

With shepherds and angels, we sing:
Glory to God and peace to all people on earth.
With Mary and Joseph we praise you, O God,
for Christ, the Word made flesh.
With joyful hearts we offer you thanks
for the gifts that grace this table.
Strengthen us with this food
that we may be witnesses to the light shining in darkness.
We ask this in the name of our Savior, Christ the Lord.
Amen

CHRISTMAS LIGHTS

Today light one white candle on the table at which you eat. On each of the Twelve Days of Christmas, add another candle until on January 6—the festival of the Epiphany—there is enough light by which to eat an early morning breakfast.

SHARING THE GIFTS OF CHRISTMAS

In England, the day after Christmas Day is called Boxing Day. Food and other treats are put into boxes and carried to friends and neighbors. This tradition reminds us to share with others the gifts we have been given. In the days and weeks ahead, consider taking food and other needed items to the local hospitality kitchen or food bank. Wash and box good usable clothing and blankets for a local shelter. Visit someone who is housebound or in prison, bringing a package of sweets, stationery, and stamps. Even very small children can help with the boxing and delivering.

First Sunday after Christmas

My eyes have seen your salvation.

LUKE 2:30

We take great care when choosing or making a gift for someone. During this season we wonder how the gifts we give are received. Is it too big for him? Will they take it back to the store? Did it make her smile? Mostly we wonder if the love we hoped to share was received with joy.

During these Christmas days we read stories about how God's gift of the Savior was received. Herod the king flew into a murderous rage. He feared Jesus would threaten his power and position. People who cling to power or wealth for life still tremble at the Gift that bids us let go of everything except God's transforming love.

Simeon was an old man who, for the length of his life, had longed to see the face of God's Messiah. Seeing Jesus, he stretched out his arms to cradle the Gift; he placed his own life and death in God's hands. The little ones of the earth—the poor, the weak, the lowly, and all who know their need of God—still receive the Messiah with open arms.

Mary and Joseph protected the child Jesus. Yet they had to learn that he was not given to them alone but to the whole world. They could not hold him too tightly nor keep him safe from pain. He was rejected because he welcomed children, ate with sinners, and loved people who were called unclean and unworthy. He suffered and died, revealing how deep God's love is, how wide God's embrace. Risen to life, he still comes as God's gift.

How do we receive the gift God gives to us, and to the world, in Jesus?

In all her newness
I watch her discover each part
and pray that eye

and ear
and hand may always be open
to know the one who fashioned them.

Babies:
God's way of retracing
the shape of the incarnation.

JAN RICHARDSON

HYMN

O little town of Bethlehem, how still we see thee lie!
Above thy deep and dreamless sleep the silent stars go by;
yet in thy dark streets shineth the everlasting light.
The hopes and fears of all the years are met in thee tonight.

For Christ is born of Mary, and, gathered all above
while mortals sleep, the angels keep their watch of wond'ring love.
O morning stars, together proclaim the holy birth,
and praises sing to God the king, and peace to all the earth!

O holy Child of Bethlehem, descend to us, we pray;
cast out our sin, and enter in, be born in us today.
We hear the Christmas angels the great glad tidings tell;
Oh, come to us, abide with us, our Lord Immanuel!

FOR READING THROUGHOUT THE WEEK

Isaiah 63:7–9	Matthew 2:13–23
Isaiah 61:10—62:3	Luke 2:22–30
1 Samuel 2:18–21	Luke 2:41–52

A PRAYER FOR THE WEEK

Lord Jesus,
in baptism we have become your brothers and sisters.
Hear us when we call to you. Come to our aid.
Amen

CHRISTMAS PRAYER FOR CHILDREN

Jesus Christ, a child so wise,
bless my hands and fill my eyes.
Watch me as I sleep in bed,
help me in the days ahead.

TABLE PRAYER

Christ is born for us! O come, let us adore him!
Lord Jesus, come to us now and bless this food and drink
so that we may be strengthened to serve your light
and speak your love in all we do.
Amen

SAYING THANK YOU

Danke, gracias, tak, eucharisto, merci, asante, domo arigato: In every
land and every language there is a way to say, "Thank you." These are
good days for writing thank-you notes to those who gave you gifts and
to those who are a gift to you. This can be a group event. Be wise stewards and use cards you have received to make new notes or create a stencil with cardboard or a cookie cutter. Take this time to thank God for
those to whom you write and to pray for them in the coming year.

The Second Sunday after Christmas

No one has ever seen God. It is God the only Son,
who is close to the Father's heart, who has made him known.
JOHN 1:18

In the beginning, when God spoke light into the darkness and life into the deep, the whole creation sang of God's goodness. People were at home with one another and with all that God had made. They tasted God's love for them in the air they breathed, the water they drank, the orchard that gave them shade by day and food when they were hungry. They saw God's beauty in the tiger running and the hummingbird humming. God's word to them was as sweet as honey: "It is good."

Later they began to hunger for another word. They no longer trusted God's goodness to be their home. So when the time was right, God's Word became flesh and lived among us: bone of our bone, breath of our breath, Jesus the Christ. Jesus had human hopes and hungers. He tasted joy and sorrow. He was ignored by some, misunderstood by others, and finally, rejected. Yet from the beginning, he knew God's heart was his home.

No one ever has seen God, but Jesus makes God known to us. Christ still comes speaking light into our darkness and our fears, life into our deep grief and our dying, even losses of the daily kind. Christ comes to make a home among us and to connect us, once again, with each other and with all living things. In his name we become children of God and receive grace upon grace. When we abide in Jesus and he in us, wherever we live, we are at home within the heart of God. Then we sing, "O taste and see that life is good, and God is very good indeed."

The world is
not with us enough.
"O taste and see"

the subway Bible poster said,
meaning the Lord,
meaning
if anything all that lives
to the imagination's tongue,

grief, mercy, language,
tangerine, weather, to
breathe them, bite,
savor, chew, swallow, transform

into our flesh our
death, crossing the street, plum, quince,
living in the orchard and being

hungry, and plucking
the fruit.

DENISE LEVERTOV

HYMN

In a lowly manger born, humble life begun in scorn;
under Joseph's watchful eye, Jesus grew as you and I;
knew the suff'rings of the weak, knew the patience of the meek,
hungered as but poor folk can; this is he. Behold the man!

Visiting the lone and lost, steadying the tempest-tossed,
giving of himself in love, calling minds to things above.
Sinners gladly hear his call; publicans before him fall,
for in him new life began; this is he. Behold the man!

Then, to rescue you and me, Jesus died upon the tree.
See in him God's love revealed; by his Passion we are healed.
Now he lives in glory bright, lives again in pow'r and might;
come and take the path he trod, Son of Mary, Son of God.

Tune: MABUNE—*other tunes are noted in the index*

FOR READING THROUGHOUT THE WEEK

Jeremiah 31:7–14	Psalm 147
Ephesians 1:3–14	John 1:10–18

A PRAYER FOR THE WEEK

God our Creator,
you have filled us with the light of the Word-made-flesh.
Let the light of our faith so shine in our lives
that others may give praise to you.
Amen

CHRISTMAS PRAYER FOR CHILDREN

I do not fear—
the Lord is near
through this dark night
as in the light.
And while I sleep
safe watch will keep.
I do not fear—
the Light is near.

TABLE PRAYER

We offer you thanks, O God,
for your Son who is our light and our life.
As we share this meal, strengthen us with your gifts
and inspire us to share our abundance with the poor.
As we go forth from this table, help us to be light
for all who live without hope.
Amen

BURNING THE CHRISTMAS TREE

In England, on Twelfth Night (January 5), many people gather with their neighbors and burn their Christmas trees in one place. In an open field, this is a large and bright bonfire. The sparks fly into the night sky like shooting stars, like the news of God's love winging its way to all peoples of every nation. If you practice this custom, make sure you do so where it is safe (and permitted) to burn trees. Take turns placing branches on the fire and naming aloud places and people around the world. This is our prayer for peace to bless the earth and God's love to be made known everywhere to everyone.

Epiphany

Arise, shine; for your light has come,
and the glory of the Lord has risen upon you.

ISAIAH 60:1

The Epiphany of the Lord

They saw the child with Mary his mother; and they knelt down
and paid him homage.

MATTHEW 2:11

An epiphany is an appearing, the revealing of something hidden. Opening a gift can be an epiphany. Meg's brother was surprised when his sister unwrapped the Christmas present from her friend, Mikki. It was a wooden apple painted red that opened in the middle. Inside were a round wooden table with three legs, three small chairs, and three tiny plates and tea cups. Meg squealed with delight. Gently she removed the pieces from the apple and set the table as if for guests.

Her brother had seen what Meg seemed not to notice: The apple was faded in places and one of the table legs had been broken and then carefully, but not perfectly, glued. He could not resist saying to her, "It looks as if Mikki already played with your present." "Of course she has," Meg replied, astonished by what her brother could not see. "So have I. Her grandpa gave it to her when she was two years old. It's her favorite toy. Now I know that I am her best friend." Pausing for emphasis, she added, "It's a Japanese tradition."

In this ancient gift-giving tradition, a person does not buy something new but gives a treasured possession of her own. Opening such a gift is an epiphany; it uncovers the hidden depths of the giver's heart. Today we celebrate the appearing of God's gift to all nations, a gift given in the Japanese tradition. Jesus is God's only begotten Son, cherished and beloved from the beginning of time. Jesus reveals to the Magi, to us, and to all peoples the very heart of God: a heart of pure, unspeakable love.

Creator of the Stars
God of Epiphanies
You are the Great Star
You have marked my path with light
You have filled my sky with stars
    naming each star
    guiding it
    until it shines upon my heart
    awakening me to deeper seeing
    new revelations
    and brighter epiphanies.

O infinite Star Giver
I now ask for wisdom and courage
    to follow these stars
    for their names are many
    and my heart is fearful.
They shine on me wherever I go:
    The Star of Hope
    The Star of Mercy and Compassion
    The Star of Justice and Peace
    The Star of Tenderness and Love
    The Star of Suffering
    The Star of Joy
And every time I feel the shine
    I am called
    to follow it
    to sing it
    to live it
    all the way to the cross
    and beyond

O Creator of the Stars
You have become within me
    an unending Epiphany.

MACRINA WIEDERKEHR

HYMN

Brightest and best of the stars of the morning,
dawn on our darkness and lend us your aid.
Stars of the East, the horizon adorning,
guide where our infant Redeemer is laid.

Shall we not yield him, in costly devotion,
fragrance of Edom and off'rings divine,
gems of the mountain and pearls of the ocean,
myrrh from the forest or gold from the mine?

Vainly we offer each ample oblation,
vainly with gifts would his favor secure;
richer by far is the heart's adoration,
dearer to God are the prayers of the poor.

Tune: MORNING STAR—*other tunes are noted in the index*

FOR READING THROUGHOUT THE WEEK

Isaiah 60:1–6   Psalm 72
Ephesians 3:1–12   Matthew 2:1–12

A PRAYER FOR THE WEEK

Lord Jesus,
you have given us many good gifts.
May our words of peace and acts of justice shed light in the darkness.
Amen

EPIPHANY PRAYER FOR CHILDREN

What can I give him,
poor as I am?
If I were a shepherd,
I would bring a lamb;
if I were a wise man
I would do my part;
yet what I can I give him—
I will give my heart.

CHRISTINA ROSETTI

TABLE PRAYER

Generous God,
you have come to us in Jesus, the light of the world.
As this food and drink give us refreshment,
strengthen us by your Spirit,
that as your baptized sons and daughters
we may share your light with all the world.
Grant this through Christ our Lord.
Amen

BLESSING OF THE HOME AT THE NEW YEAR OR ON EPIPHANY

Matthew writes that when the wise men saw the shining star stop overhead, they were filled with joy. "On entering the house, they saw the child with Mary his mother" (2:10–11). In the home, Christ is met in family and friends, in visitors and strangers. In the home, faith is shared, nurtured, and put into action. In the home, Christ is welcome. Whether you live alone or with others, you may invite friends and other family members to gather for this blessing followed by refreshments or a festive meal. Someone may lead with the greeting and blessing while someone else may read the text from scripture. In eastern European countries, Christians add a visual blessing on or over the main door. It is written with white chalk; for example, 20+C+M+B+01. The numbers change with each new year. The three letters stand for either the ancient Latin blessing *Christe mansionem benedica*, which means, "Christ, bless this house," or the legendary names of the Magi (Caspar, Melchior, and Balthasar).

GREETING

May peace be to this house
and to all who enter here.
By wisdom a house is built
and through understanding it is established;
through knowledge its rooms are filled with rare and beautiful treasures.

see PROVERBS 24:3-4

SCRIPTURE READING

As we prepare to ask God's blessing on this household,
let us listen to the words of scripture.

In the beginning was the Word,
and the Word was with God, and the Word was God.
He was in the beginning with God.
All things came into being through him,
and without him not one thing came into being.
What has come into being in him was life,
and the life was the light of all people.
The Word became flesh and lived among us,
and we have seen his glory,
the glory as of a father's only son, full of grace and truth.
From his fullness we have all received, grace upon grace.

JOHN 1:1-4, 14, 16

PRAYER OF BLESSING

O God,
you revealed your Son to all people
by the shining light of a star.
We pray that you bless this home and all who live here
with your gracious presence.
May your love be our inspiration,
your wisdom our guide,
your truth our light,
and your peace our benediction;
through Christ our Lord.
Amen

LIGHTS AND GIFTS

Twelve candles now burn on the table, making enough light by which to eat a pre-dawn breakfast. Some families or individuals feast on a large breakfast "fit for kings and queens."

This is also a day for giving gifts. In Russia, the Magi or Kings leave gifts for the children in the house, honoring every child as they once honored the child Jesus. Consider giving something you cherish to someone you love, and do it in secret!

The Baptism of the Lord

Here is my servant whom I uphold;
he will bring forth justice to the nations.

ISAIAH 42:1

We thank God for water. Water splashing down rocks high in the mountains. Rain softening the fields, dew making damp the meadows. Oceans for whales, lakes for trout, and rivers that run to the sea. Water for drinking, bathing, and diving. Water for life. We thank God for nourishing and sustaining us and all living things with water.

We thank God for the Word. The Word of promise spoken to Jesus at the River Jordan: "You are my beloved Son." See the epiphany: Jesus, born of Mary and baptized by John, is revealed as God's only begotten son. This same Word is spoken at our baptism: "You are God's child, chosen and cherished." Hear the epiphany: We thank God for the Word-bound water that washes us and runs like a river of promise through all our days.

We thank God for the Holy Spirit. In the beginning, when God created the world, the Spirit swept over the face of the waters. In the fullness of time, the Spirit brooded over Mary's womb-waters and a new creation came to life: Jesus Christ. At the Jordan, the Spirit descended upon Jesus and led him out of the river and into the wilderness where he struggled with the powers that tried to separate him from God. On Pentecost, the Spirit danced like fire-flames upon the followers of Jesus, enkindling a community to declare the mighty acts of God and serve the world in Jesus' name. We thank God for the Spirit who stirs us to life and leads us through every trial toward the cross and into Easter joy.

We thank God for the Word-bound, Spirit-stirred water of our new birth.

The columbine and glacier lilies grow
in patches cleared by some forgotten slide,
an avalanche of grinding rock and snow
that roared with sudden vengeance down the side

of Martin's Ridge, just short of Holden Lake.
The waters leap like divers from a bridge,
urged by sun to plunge, the sun that bakes
the rocks and slowly hammers down the ridge.

And still the flowers thrive, they push along,
rooted inside the earth, but not bowed down,
ascending from the valley like a song.
I hear and see, I dive and I am drowned:

As driven from behind, or called ahead,
to break the waters, risen from the dead.

TIM GUSTAFSON

HYMN

Wash, O God, our sons and daughters, where your cleansing waters flow.
Number them among your people; bless as Christ blessed long ago.
Weave them garments bright and sparkling; compass them with love and light.
Fill, anoint them; send your Spirit, holy dove and heart's delight.

We who bring them long for nurture; by your milk may we be fed.
Let us join your feast, partaking cup of blessing, living bread.
God, renew us, guide our footsteps; free from sin and all its snares,
one with Christ in living, dying, by your Spirit, children, heirs.

Oh, how deep your holy wisdom! Unimagined, all your ways!
To your name be glory, honor! With our lives we worship, praise!
We your people stand before you, water-washed and Spirit-born.
By your grace, our lives we offer. Recreate us; God, transform!

Tune: BEACH SPRING—*other tunes are noted in the index*

FOR READING THROUGHOUT THE WEEK

Isaiah 42:1–9	Matthew 3:13–17
Genesis 1:1–5	Mark 1:4–11
Isaiah 43:1–7	Luke 3:15–22

A PRAYER FOR THE WEEK

Holy God, you have given us birth in the waters of baptism.
May your Spirit strengthen us to be your witnesses. Amen

EPIPHANY PRAYER FOR CHILDREN

Christ be with me, Christ within me,
Christ behind me, Christ before me,
Christ beside me, Christ to win me,
Christ to comfort and restore me.

TABLE PRAYER

O good and gracious God,
we praise you for the light of Christ
that shines in our midst.
Receive our thanks for the gifts of this table
and strengthen us with your love
that we may be light
for those who dwell in darkness and the shadows of death.
Grant this through Christ our Lord.
Amen

THANKSGIVING FOR BAPTISM

The celebration of the Lord's baptism is the occasion on which many Christians renew their baptismal promises. In some countries, this is accompanied by water-related activities and games. In Spain, water is splashed on unsuspecting individuals; in Ethiopia, people swim in pools and rivers, refreshing themselves in God's gift of water. A simple way to renew one's baptism into Christ is to gather around a bowl of water and a burning candle. Use this prayer.

Lord Jesus,
the light of a star led the Magi to you.
Help us guide others to your unfading light.

Lord Jesus,
in the River Jordan you were proclaimed God's beloved child.
Strengthen us in our baptism as your brothers and sisters.

Lord Jesus,
you have brought us through the waters of death to new life.
Renew in us the power of your Spirit so that we may follow you in peace.

Lord Jesus,
you were anointed by the Spirit to bring good news to the afflicted.
Give us the grace to serve all those in need.
Amen

The Transfiguration of the Lord

This is my Son, the Beloved; listen to him.

MARK 9:7

All of Advent, Christmas, and Epiphany have led us to this mountain and this moment. Once again we hear God speak, "You are my beloved son, my chosen one." We see a vision glorious, another epiphany: Jesus is bathed in the light of heaven, the glory of God shines upon him. Moses, the law-giver, and Elijah, the prophet, fade and disappear. All that has been finds its fullness here. The disciples are told to listen to Jesus and follow him. All that is to come finds its source here. On this mountain, in this moment, there is Jesus only.

From a mountain top we can see both where we have been and where we are going. Looking back we remember the hope and expectation of Advent, the joy and celebration of Christmas, the surprise and wonder of Epiphany. Looking forward we see the way that leads to Jerusalem and to another mountain that holds the cross. God's love revealed to us in Jesus is seen most clearly on the cross, where loving the world to love's fullest, he laid down his life for his friends.

We will go with Jesus to Jerusalem, to Gethsemane, and to Golgatha. We know the way, we have traveled this season before. When the noonday sun darkens on that Friday we call good, we will prepare in faith for God's last great Epiphany. Then we will run to the Feast of the Resurrection, the mountain peak from which we see God's future: all nations singing, all peoples feasting, all creation united in Christ. In every season, on every Sunday, we return—as if for the first time—to this mountain, this moment, this feast.

Suddenly, they saw him the way he was,
the way he really was all the time,
although they had never seen it before,
the glory which blinds the everyday eye
and so becomes invisible. This is how
he was, radiant, brilliant, carrying joy
like a flaming sun in his hands.
This is the way he was-is-from the beginning,
and we cannot bear it. So he manned himself,
came manifest to us; and there on the mountain
they saw him, really saw him, saw his light.
We all know that if we really see him we die.
But isn't that what is required of us?
Then, perhaps, we will see each other, too.

MADELEINE L'ENGLE

HYMN

O Light of Light, love given birth;
Jesus, Redeemer of the earth:
more bright than day your face did show,
your raiment whiter than the snow.

Two prophets, who had faith to see,
with your elect found company;
the heavens above your glory named,
your Father's voice his Son proclaimed.

May all who seek to praise aright
through purer lives show forth your light.
To you, the King of glory, now
all faithful hearts adoring bow.

tune: JESU DULCIS MEMORIA—*other tunes are noted in the index.*

FOR READING THROUGHOUT THE WEEK

Exodus 24:12–18   Matthew 17:1–9
2 Kings 2:1–12   Mark 9:2–9
Exodus 34:29–35   Luke 9:28–43

A PRAYER FOR THE WEEK

O God, in the transfiguration of your Son we see your gracious light.
Give us the grace to live as children of the light. Amen

EPIPHANY PRAYER FOR CHILDREN

I want to walk as a child of the light.
I want to follow Jesus.
God set the stars to give light to the world.
The star of my life is Jesus.

TABLE PRAYER

Arise, shine, your light has come.
The glory of God has risen upon you.
May the food and drink which we bless in your name,
O Lord, give us strength to walk as children of the light.
Amen

PREPARING FOR CARNIVAL

In many parts of the world, Christians end the Epiphany season and
prepare for Lent by holding a party on the Tuesday before Ash Wednes-
day. This day has different names: Shrove Tuesday, Mardi Gras, Carnival.
It is time to enjoy cakes, doughnuts, pancakes, and other sweet baked
goods. This is no time to count calories! But when your party or festive
meal is over, it will be time to remove all the remaining decorations in
the home associated with the season of light. It is time to prepare the
household for Lent. It is a day of turning.

Hymn Index

"Come, thou long-expected Jesus" may be sung to HOLY MANNA ("God, who stretched the spangled heavens"), HYFRYDOL ("Love divine, all loves excelling"), or JESU, JOY OF MAN'S DESIRING ("Come with us, O blessed Jesus").

"Hark, the glad sound! The Savior comes" may be sung to CONSOLATION ("The king shall come when morning dawns"), LAND OF REST ("Jerusalem, my happy home"), or ST. ANNE ("O God, our help in ages past").

"Your little ones, dear Lord, are we" may be sung to MARYTON ("O Master, let me walk with you"), OLD HUNDREDTH ("Praise God, from whom all blessings flow"), or TALLIS' CANON ("All praise to thee, my God, this night").

"In a lowly manger born" may be sung to SALZBURG ("Songs of thankfulness and praise") or ST. GEORGE'S, WINDSOR ("Come, you thankful people, come").

"Brightest and best of the stars of the morning" may be sung to O PERFECT LOVE ("O perfect Love, all human thought transcending") or CITY OF GOD ("O Jesus Christ, may grateful hymns be rising").

"Wash, O God, our sons and daughters" may be sung to ABBOTT'S LEIGH ("Lord, you give the great commission"), HYFRYDOL ("Love divine, all loves excelling"), or JESU, JOY OF MAN'S DESIRING ("Come with us, O blessed Jesus").

"O Light of Light" may be sung to OLD HUNDREDTH ("Praise God, from whom all blessings flow") or TALLIS' CANON ("All praise to thee, my God, this night").

Acknowledgments

Angels gather
"Arrival" from *Shaker, Why Don't You Sing?* by Maya Angelou, copyright © 1983 Maya Angelou. Used by permission of Random House, Inc.

Come, thou long-expected Jesus
Text by Charles Wesley; public domain.

God in the night
From *The Promise of His Glory,* copyright © The Central Board of Finance of The Church of England. Used by permission of The Liturgical Press.

Here I wait
Author unknown.

When the King shall come again
Text by Christopher Idle. Text copyright © 1982 Hope Publishing Co., Carol Stream, IL 60188. All rights reserved. Used by permission.

i thank You God
By e.e. cummings. Copyright © 1950, © 1978, 1991 Trustees for the E.E. Cummings Trust. Copyright © 1979 George James Firmage, from *Complete Poems: 1904–1962* by e.e. cummings, edited by George J. Firmage. Used by permission of Liveright Publishing Corporation.

Hark, the glad sound! The Savior comes
Text by Philip Doddridge; public domain.

There stood in heaven
Dutch carol. Text translated by G.R. Woodward; public domain.

O come, O Wisdom from on high
O come, O come, Emmanuel; public domain.

Angel sent by God to guide me
public domain.

Infant holy, infant lowly
public domain.